MAPLE RIDGE ELEMENTARY SCHOOL
20820 - River Road
MAPLE RIDGE, B. C.

796.9

HER

ACTION SPORTS
SKIING

Joe Herran and Ron Thomas

Philadelphia

This edition first published in 2004 in the United States of America by Chelsea House Publishers, a subsidiary of Haights Cross Communications.

All rights reserved. No part of this publication may be reproduced or transmitted in any form or by any means without the written permission of the publisher.

Chelsea House Publishers
1974 Sproul Road, Suite 400
Broomall, PA 19008-0914

The Chelsea House world wide web address is www.chelseahouse.com

Library of Congress Cataloging-in-Publication Data

Herran, Joe.
 Skiing / Joe Herran and Ron Thomas.
 p. cm. — (Action sports)

 Includes index.
 Contents: Introduction — What is skiing? — Skiing gear — Skiing safely — Skills and techniques — The ski resort — In competition — Skiing champions — Then and now — Related action sports — Glossary — Index.

 ISBN 0-7910-7537-0
 1. Skiing—Juvenile literature. [1. Skiing.] I. Thomas, Ron, 1947–
 II. Title. III. Series: Action sports (Chelsea House Publishers).
 GV854.315.H47 2004
 796.93—dc21

2003001183

First published in 2003 by
MACMILLAN EDUCATION AUSTRALIA PTY LTD
627 Chapel Street, South Yarra, Australia, 3141

Associated companies and representatives throughout the world.

Copyright © Joe Herran and Ron Thomas 2003
Copyright in photographs © individual photographers as credited

Edited by Renée Otmar, Otmar Miller Consultancy Pty Ltd, Melbourne
Text and cover design by Karen Young
Illustration by Nives Porcellato and Andy Craig
Page layout by Raul Diche
Photo research by Legend Images

Printed in China

Acknowledgements
The author and the publisher are grateful to the following for permission to reproduce copyright materials:

Cover photograph: downhill alpine skier in midair, courtesy of Corbis Digital Stock.

AP/Wide World Photos, p. 27 (center); Australian Picture Library/Corbis, pp. 28–29 (center), 29 (right); Corbis Digital Stock, pp. 8, 10, 19; Falls Creek Ski School, pp. 6, 7, 9, 15, 16 (bottom), 17; Getty Images, pp. 4, 5, 14, 16 (top), 18, 20–21 (top), 21, 22, 27 (left), 30; Legend Images, p. 13; Mitchell Library, State Library of New South Wales, p. 28 (left); Perisher Blue, p. 23 (bottom); Perisher Blue, photo by Steve Cuff, p. 23 (top); Reuters, pp. 11, 24, 25, 26, 27 (right).

While every care has been taken to trace and acknowledge copyright, the publisher tenders their apologies for any accidental infringement where copyright has proved untraceable. Where the attempt has been unsuccessful, the publisher welcomes information that would redress the situation.

CONTENTS

Introduction	4
What is skiing?	5
Skiing gear	6
Skiing safely	12
Skills and techniques	14
The ski resort	22
In competition	24
Skiing champions	26
Then and now	28
Related action sports	30
Glossary	31
Index	32

INTRODUCTION

In this book you will read about:
- the skis and other gear used by skiers
- the safety measures used to keep skiers safe
- the basic skills and styles of skiing
- ski resorts
- some of the top skiers in competition today
- the history of the sport from its beginnings in ancient times.

In the beginning

Skiing began thousands of years ago. Rock carvings in Norway from 4,500 years ago show a man hunting with long, ski-like runners on his feet. Ancient writings tell of Viking kings who were great skiers about 2,000 years ago.

In the 1700s and 1800s, soldiers in the armies of Norway and Sweden wore skis when they fought during the winter months.

Skiing was introduced into the United States in the 1830s, and into Australia in the 1860s by Norwegian miners who used thick wooden skis to travel over snow and for leisure skiing. By the 1890s, skiing had become a popular winter sport and ski races were regular events.

Skiing today

Modern design and the use of **carbon fiber** and fiberglass have led to the development of improved, lighter skis and ski poles. Ski clothing, too, is lighter and more durable. Skiing competition is part of the Winter Olympics.

 **Warning** This is not a how-to book for aspiring skiers. It is intended as an introduction to the exciting world of skiing, and a look at where the sport has come from and where it is heading.

WHAT IS SKIING?

Skiing is gliding over the snow with the feet strapped to skis. Ski poles are used by skiers for balance and to increase speed. There are four main types of skiing:

- alpine skiing
- nordic skiing
- freestyle
- free skiing.

Alpine skiing

Alpine skiing includes **downhill** skiing and **slalom**. Downhill skiers ski as fast as they can to reach the bottom of the slope.

Nordic skiing

Nordic skiing includes cross-country skiing and ski jumping. Cross-country skiers travel through fields, forests and along trails. Ski jumpers speed down a ramp called an inrun, and at the end of it take off to become airborne before landing.

Freestyle

The two kinds of **freestyle skiing** are called aerials and **moguls**. Aerial skiers perform acrobatics on their skis after taking off from a ramp called a kicker. In mogul skiing, skiers ski at high speed down a bumpy slope, jumping, spinning and turning as often as possible.

Free skiing

Free skiing is for those skiers who want to explore the countryside away from the ski resorts.

> **ACTION FACT**
> Skiing originated in Norway. The words "ski" and "slalom" are in fact Norwegian.

Slalom skiers zigzag downhill, changing direction quickly to ski around flags called **gates** that are set in the snow.

Mogul skiers combine acrobatics with high speed.

SKIING GEAR

The skis

Skis generally are built in layers around a core of foam plastic or wood. The core is designed to absorb vibrations. Layers of fiberglass, carbon fiber or metal are used to cover the core and give it strength. The base is made from **polyethylene**, which slides easily over snow. The **edges** are made of sharp, stainless steel to give the ski strength and to cut into the snow.

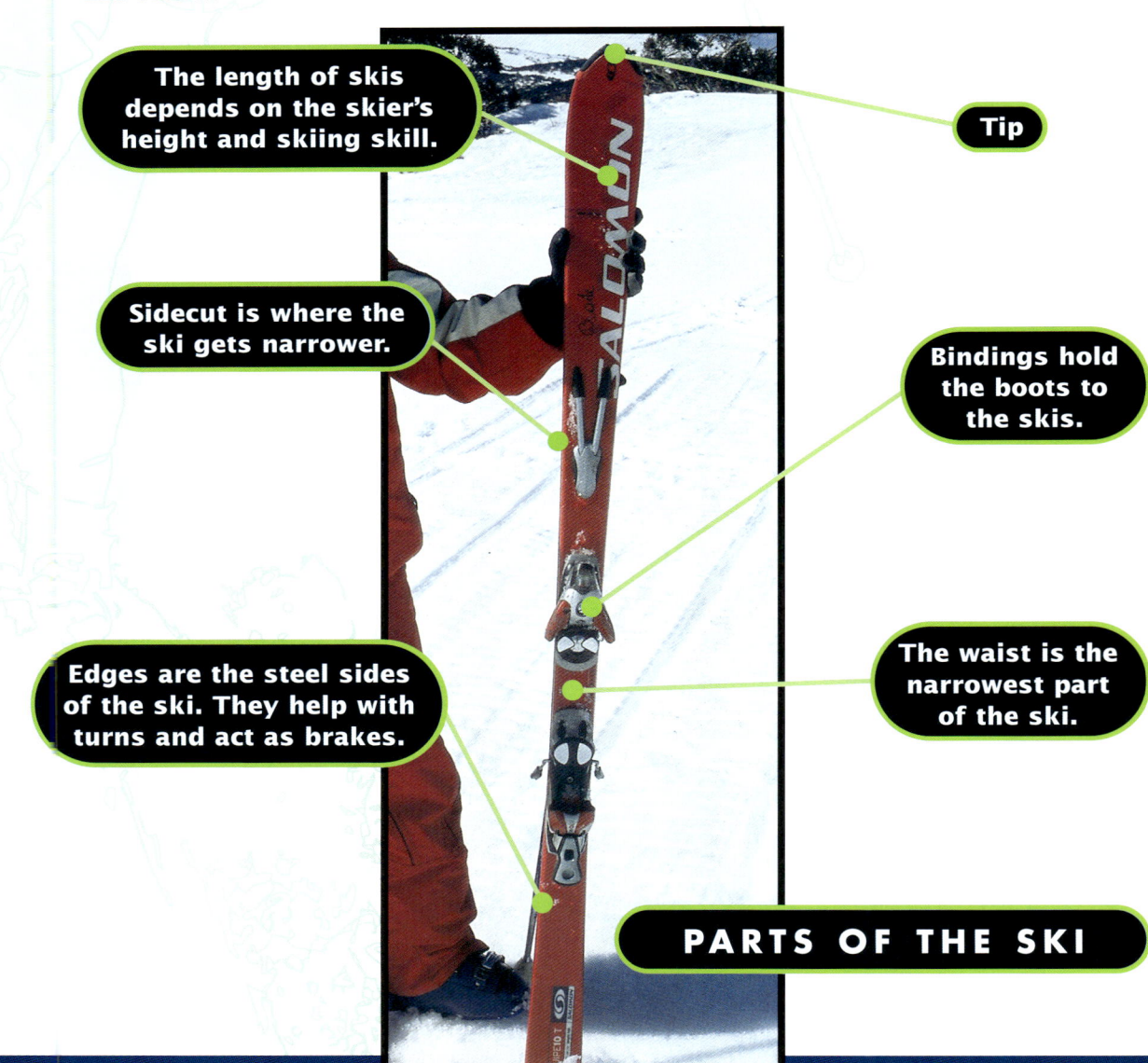

- The length of skis depends on the skier's height and skiing skill.
- Tip
- Sidecut is where the ski gets narrower.
- Bindings hold the boots to the skis.
- Edges are the steel sides of the ski. They help with turns and act as brakes.
- The waist is the narrowest part of the ski.

PARTS OF THE SKI

Slalom skis

Slalom skis are short for quick turning. They have a deep sidecut.

Downhill and cross-country skis

Downhill and cross-country skis are designed to go straight and fast, so have very little sidecut. Cross-country skis are fitted to be about 8 to 12 inches (20 to 30 centimeters) longer than the skier's height. They are also cambered (arched) so that when the skier is gliding along, the foot is clear of the snow.

Other skis

Free skiers and extreme skiers use long, fat skis that float quickly through powder snow.

Maintaining the skis

The base of the skis must be kept perfectly flat and as clean and smooth as possible. A cleaning fluid is used to remove dirt from the base. Hot **wax** is then poured onto the skis and smoothed with an iron. When the wax has cooled a little, it is scraped to leave a smooth, fine layer of wax. Waxing the skis makes them run faster and turn easily, as well as making them waterproof.

Edges grip the snow and help the skier to make turns. If the edges are rounded or burred, they will slip and make turning difficult, so edges are filed to keep them sharp for icy conditions.

Skis come in all colors. They are usually decorated with graphics designed by ski companies.

Ski poles

Ski poles help a skier keep balance and increase speed. The shafts are usually made of a light metal such as aluminum. The end of the pole is called the point and the metal or plastic disk above the point, which stops the pole from sinking into the snow, is called the basket. The skier puts his or her hands through the handle straps and holds the pole at the grip. When gripping ski poles that are the correct size, the skier's forearms will be horizontal to the body.

Bindings

Bindings hold the skier's boots to the skis. The skier steps into the bindings and clicks down to secure the boots. If the skier falls, the bindings release the skis from the boots. When the bindings release, the brake springs back down to stop the ski from sliding down the mountain and causing injury to other skiers.

Ski poles help the skier to balance.

There are three parts to the bindings:
- the heel piece, which releases and opens in a forward fall
- the toe piece, which releases sideways in a twisting fall
- brakes, which lift out of the snow when the skier steps into the bindings.

Boots

Boots hold the skier's feet firmly on the skis. They should fit well and be comfortable. Boots are made of a rigid **polyurethane** shell, and have soft, padded inner linings, which can be removed for washing and drying.

ACTION FACT

Cross-country skiers wear shoes like running shoes. Only the tip of the toe is held by the bindings.

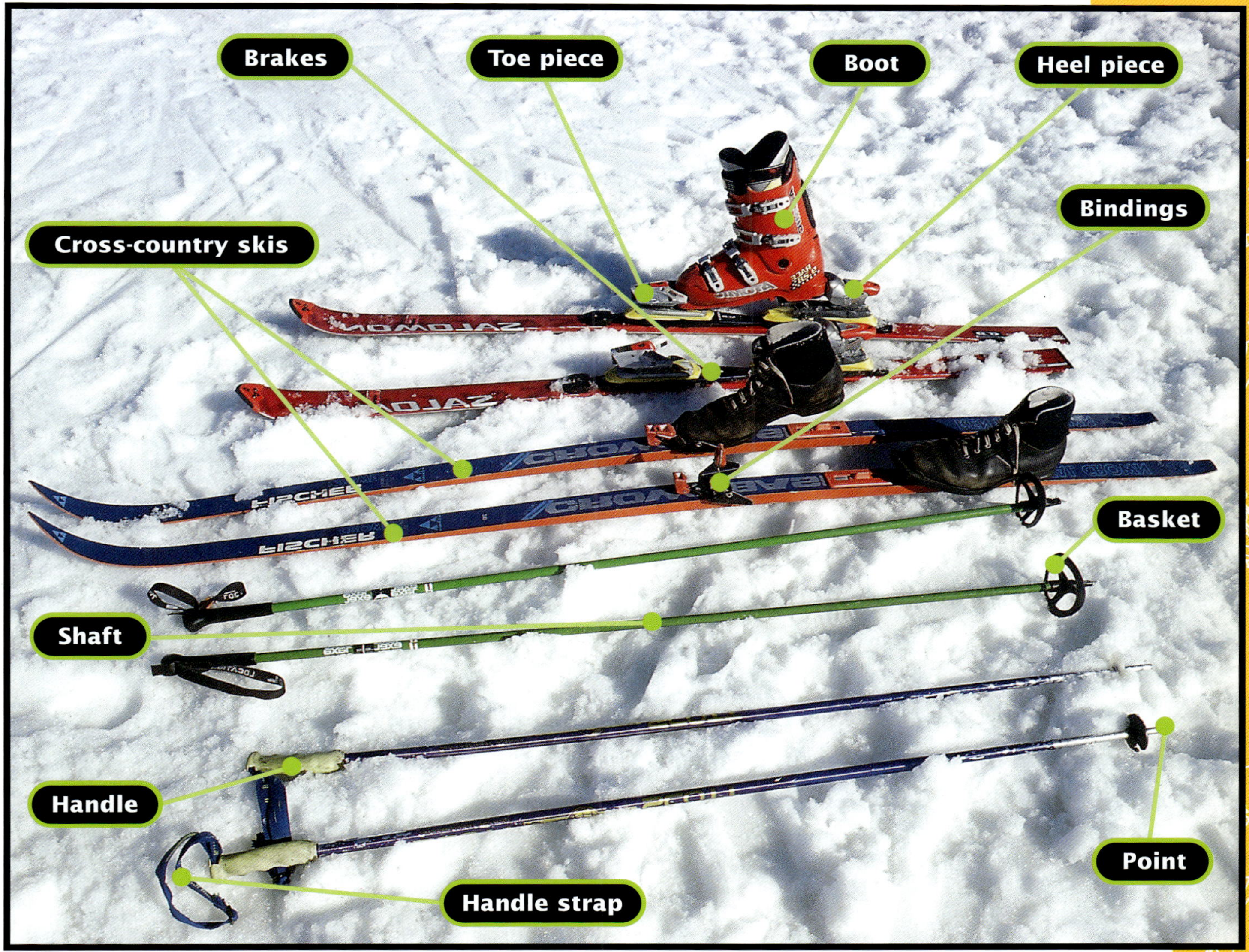

- Brakes
- Toe piece
- Boot
- Heel piece
- Cross-country skis
- Bindings
- Basket
- Shaft
- Handle
- Point
- Handle strap

Other gear

Clothes

Ski clothes are made of material that is hard-wearing, lightweight, waterproof and insulated against the cold. Skiers usually wear layers of clothes to keep out the cold. The first layer is often a pair of thermal underpants with long legs (long johns) and a thermal vest. This special underwear absorbs perspiration and traps warm air next to the body. The outer layer is a jacket and pants with air vents that can be opened and closed with a zipper, depending on whether the skier feels hot or cold.

Gloves

Skiers wear gloves with cuffs that fit over the sleeves of their jackets. These keep their hands warm and dry. Gloves worn by ski racers have extra padding across the back and in the wrists to protect the hands from damage on downhill slalom races through gates.

- Woollen beanie or cap
- Goggles or sunglasses
- Waterproof jacket with air vents
- Gloves
- Waterproof pants

Head gear

Head gear is worn because body heat is lost through the head. A woollen beanie or cap will keep a skier's head warm.

A helmet is worn by skiers tackling free skiing, ski jumping and extreme forms of skiing. Helmets are lightweight and are designed to provide protection against the cold. A skier wearing a correctly fitting helmet is safe and comfortable and can see and hear clearly.

Goggles or sunglasses

Goggles or sunglasses help skiers to see better in the glare of the snow. They also keep flying snow and wind out of their eyes. They will protect the skier's eyes from the sun's harmful ultraviolet (UV) rays. UV rays are more intense high up a mountain, even on a dull day.

Skiers prefer goggles or sunglasses with plastic lenses. They are lighter and do not break into dangerous splinters, as glass lenses do. The lenses are also specially treated to resist fogging.

Sunscreen and lip protector

Sunscreen and lip protector are used by skiers to protect their skin from harmful rays of the sun.

ACTION FACT

Hypothermia is an extreme loss of body heat that occurs when a person gets too cold. The person becomes tired, lacks the energy to keep moving, and may collapse.

Slalom skiers wear a lightweight helmet, goggles and gloves.

SKIING SAFELY

Skiing is a fun sport, but it can also be dangerous because of the many hazards that surround skiers in cold, snowy country.

Obeying the rules

Skiers should follow these basic rules to keep themselves and others safe and injury-free:

- obey rules and signs
- give way to a skier who is farther downhill
- never stop on a slope or below the crest of a hill
- keep control of the skis
- never ski on slopes that are too difficult
- ski with a friend or where there are other people around
- ski within the boundaries of the ski resort to avoid getting lost
- wear protective clothing and keep warm
- check the weather conditions before skiing and watch for sudden and dangerous weather changes.

Choosing the right trail

Three internationally recognized signs help skiers to choose a trail that suits their skill level.

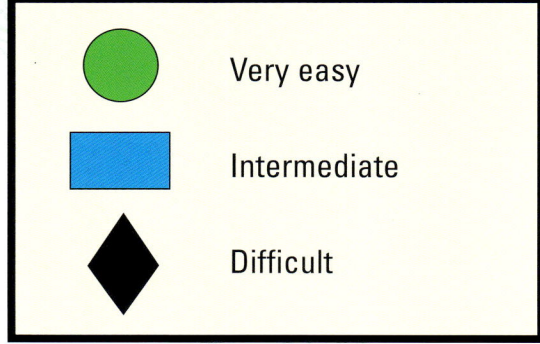

Warming up and keeping fit

Skiing is a tough sport and skiers need to be fit. To build the necessary fitness level, many skiers run, ride a bike or jump rope. Like most athletes, skiers warm up before beginning. They spend a few minutes stretching to warm up the main muscle groups in the legs and back, wrists and shoulders. Walking around, jogging on the spot or climbing for a few minutes will also warm the muscles. Warm, relaxed muscles are less likely to cramp in the cold.

ACTION FACT

Avalanches are huge slabs of snow falling down a mountain. When skiing in areas that are steep, far away from regular ski slopes, skiers should carry an avalanche transceiver. This device will send a signal to rescuers should the skier be trapped or buried in the snow.

Skiers in rough country away from the slopes of the resort need extra provisions for safety. They need to carry a first-aid kit, food, water, a map and a compass.

SKILLS AND TECHNIQUES

The basics

Most beginner skiers take lessons from a ski instructor, starting out on a gentle hill rather than a steep mountain. The skier first learns to stand on the skis with the feet shoulder-width apart and with the weight forward and balanced on both feet. Knees are slightly bent, arms are forward and the head is up.

Walking on skis

Pushing on the poles with each arm, the skier leans forward and slides the skis forward in short steps, one ski at a time. The skis glide across the snow.

Skiers slide the skis forward in short steps and push on the poles to walk on their skis.

Side-stepping up a hill

Standing with skis across the **fall line** stops the skier from sliding down the hill. To walk up a hill, the skier steps up one ski at a time. The uphill ski is moved first, then the downhill ski is lifted and placed beside the first. The movement is repeated until the skier is up the hill.

Herringbone step up a hill

The skier points the **tips** of the skis away from each other in an "open scissors" position and moves up the hill one step at a time. The skier pushes down with the knees to make the skis' inside edges dig into the snow. The herringbone step gets its name from the pattern left in the snow as the skier walks uphill.

↗ Ski poles are used for balance as the skier side-steps up a hill.

↙ The skier pushes down on the top of the ski pole handle during the herringbone step.

Beyond the basics

Learning to fall

All skiers fall at one time or another. Learning to fall safely is an important skill that will help avoid injuries. A falling skier should try to sit down with her feet together, toward one side of the skis, and bring the skis across the slope. Ski poles should be kept away from the body.

Getting up again

To get up after a fall, the skier sits just uphill from the skis with knees bent and brings the body close to the skis. The skis are across the fall line and on their edges. Both poles are placed above the uphill ski. The skier pushes down on the poles and up into a standing position.

↗ A falling skier tries to sit beside the skis, not on top of them.

↘ Getting up on skis after a fall can be difficult, and skiers should take their time.

Turning

The skier first learns to turn on flat ground, taking several steps to change direction.

- **Star turning**

  Keeping the **tail** of the ski on the snow, the tip of one ski is lifted and placed out to the side. The skier puts weight on the first ski, lifts the tip of the other ski and places it beside the first. The movements are repeated until the skier has turned around. The pattern in the snow looks like a star, which is how the turn gets its name.

- **Kick turning**

  Using the poles for support, the skier stands with skis parallel across the fall line. The skier swings the downhill ski off the snow and places its tail on the snow next to the tip of the other ski. Then the ski is swung back onto the snow, facing in the opposite direction. The skier twists their body to swing the second ski around, placing it alongside the first. The skier is now facing the other way.

STAR TURNING

KICK TURNING

Snowplowing

The snowplow is a technique that helps a skier to control speed. Using the snowplow a beginner skier can ski forward, slow down without changing direction, turn and brake.

The skier stands with knees bent, leaning slightly forward and with the weight balanced on both feet. The tips of the skis are close together and the tails are out to form a V. Poles are held pointing behind the skier. The skier can now glide down the fall line in snowplow stance.

To brake, the skier shifts weight to the skis' inside edges and pushes out with the heels to widen the space between the tails. The wider the plow the faster the stop. The poles are brought forward to help the stop.

To turn to the right, the skier shifts weight to the left foot. To turn left, the weight is shifted to the right foot. The skier looks in the direction of the turn, arms wide and poles helping with balance.

↗ The snowplow is a good skiing technique for beginners. Young skiers often practice without poles while learning the technique.

Schussing

Schussing is skiing straight downhill. The skier keeps the legs straight and bends slightly at the waist. Looking ahead, the skier steers the skis gently with the feet, keeping them parallel and pointing downhill.

To schuss over bumps in the snow, the skier learns to absorb the shock of the bump by leaning forward and flexing ankles, knees and hips as the skis cross the bumps. The upper body should be relaxed.

↗ By shifting weight from one ski to another, a skier stays in balance at all times.

Traversing

Traversing is skiing back and forth across the slope or fall line. It is a good way for a skier to control speed while descending a slope. With skis pointing across the fall line, and edged into the slope, the skier leans out slightly from the slope to place weight on the downhill ski. The skier looks ahead and slightly downhill.

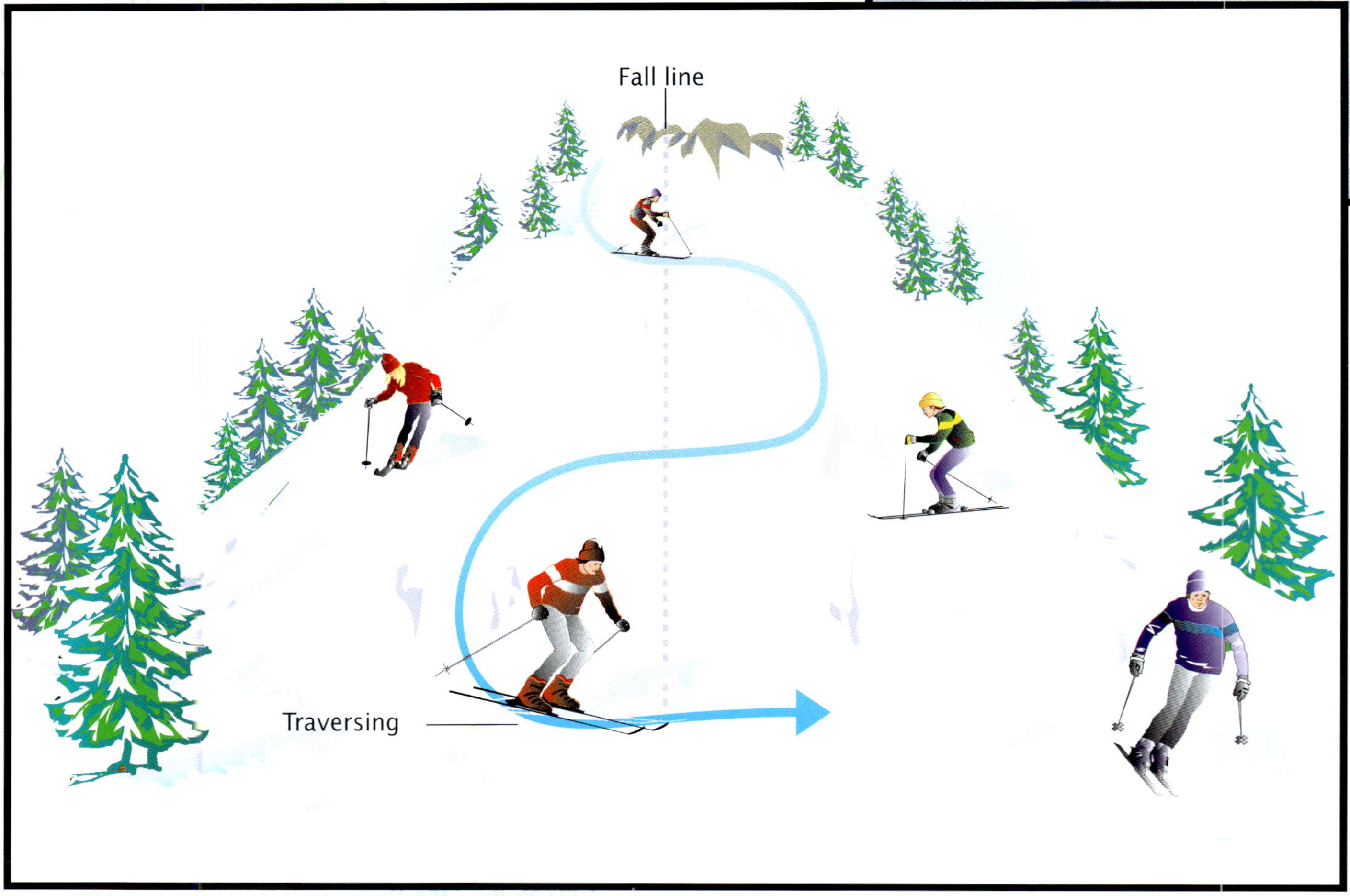

Sideslipping

Sideslipping is letting the skis slip sideways straight down the fall line. The skier controls the speed of the fall by using the skis' uphill edges to dig into the snow. Starting with skis pointing across the fall line and with weight on the downhill ski, the skier leans out away from the slope and loosens the edge on the skis. As they flatten, the skis will start to slip down the slope. To stop a sideslip, the skier shifts his weight and sinks down, rolling the knees back toward the mountain to make the uphill edges bite into the snow.

Sideslipping lets a skier move quickly down a slope without changing direction.

Carving is for expert skiers and racers.

Carving

Carving is high-speed turning on the skis' edges. Before pushing off, the skier bends the knees and puts their weight as far forward as possible. With the weight forward and knees bent into the slope, the skis will be on an edge.

During the downhill run, the skier keeps the knees bent and the shoulders square and faces down the hill at all times. The hands are kept together, low and in front of the body.

THE SKI RESORT

At the ski resort, beginner skiers spend most of their time on the gentle bunny slopes, where they learn the basics of skiing under the supervision of an instructor.

Many people take ski lessons to learn the basics and to learn new techniques.

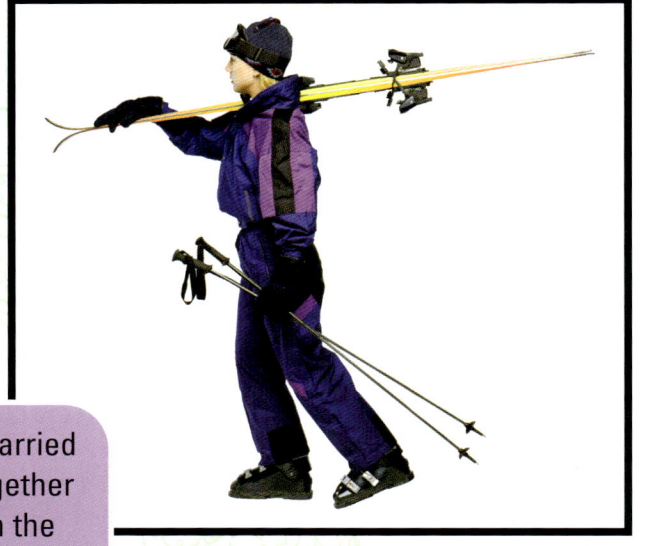

Skis are carried locked together and balanced on the skier's shoulders.

Chair lifts can be one, two, three or four seats wide.

The chair lift

A chair lift is used to move skiers quickly and safely above the **piste**, or ski runs. To board the chair lift, the skiers stand with their backs to the chair. As the chair approaches, the skiers grab the center bar and sit down, keeping the tips of the skis up.

T-Bar ski lift

A T-Bar ski lift is like an upside-down "T" hanging from a ski lift cable. The skiers, with skis riding on the ground, are pulled uphill by the bar, which is behind their backsides. Skiers often ride a T-Bar two at a time, with the stem of the "T" between them. At the top of the slope, the skiers dismount and ski away.

Maps

Ski resorts provide maps showing the mountains, the ski runs and also the location of ski schools, restaurants, ski shops and first-aid centers.

ACTION FACT

In 2002, Ski Dome, an indoor ski slope, opened in Sydney, Australia. Skiers ski downhill on a 574-foot (175-meter) diameter, 164-foot (50-meter) wide rotating slope covered with artificial snow.

T-BAR SKI LIFT

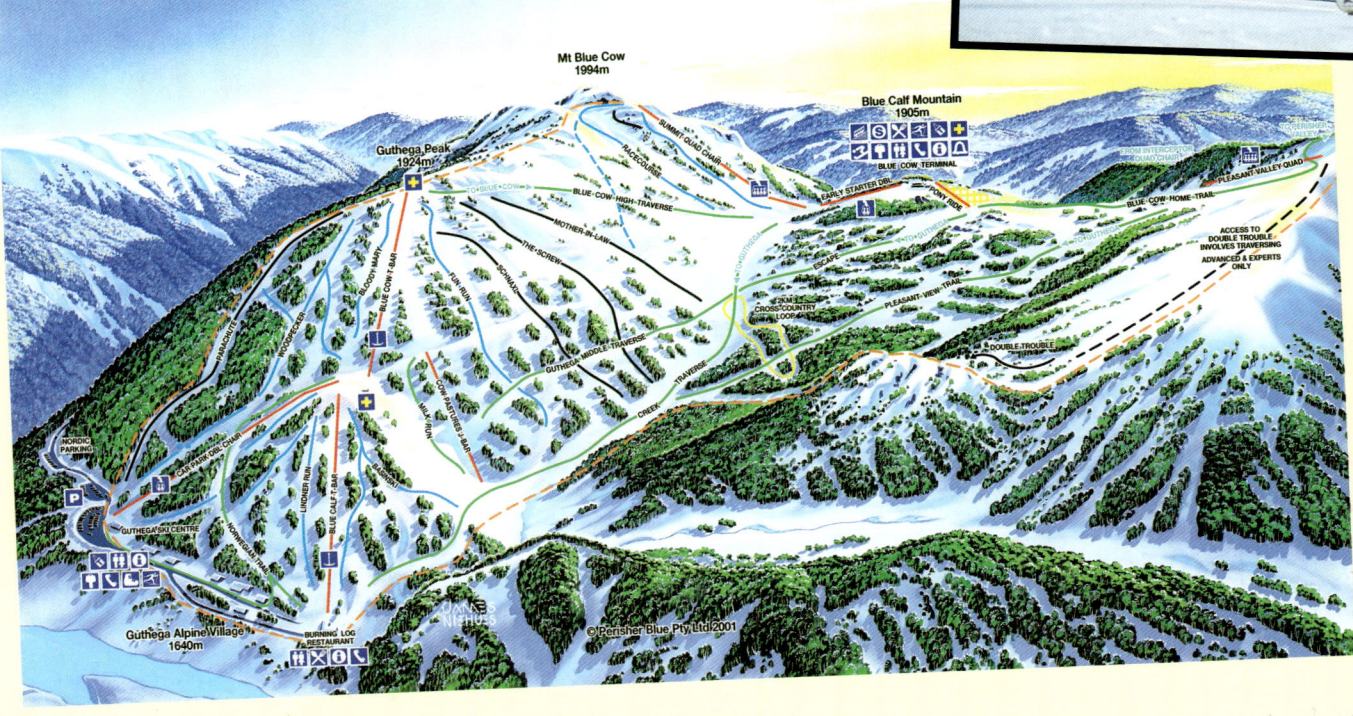

A SKI RESORT MAP

IN COMPETITION

The Fédération Internationale de Ski (FIS) organizes all major competitive ski events, including the Olympic Games skiing competition. Every year, FIS organizes a series of events for both men and women in all categories of skiing competition, including alpine, nordic and freestyle. These events take place throughout the year and around the world. At the end of the year, the skier with the most points is ranked number one in the world. FIS also organizes a World Championship event in all categories every second year, and the winner of that competition is crowned World Champion in his or her event.

At the Olympic Games, skiing competition includes a number of different events.

> **ACTION FACT**
> The record for the longest ski jump in competition is held by Andreas Goldberger (Austria), who jumped 738 feet (225 meters) in 2000.

Alpine skiing

Alpine skiing includes five events for men and women. They are:

- the downhill, where skiers race, one at a time, down a mountain course 1.8 to 2.5 miles (3 to 4 kilometers) long. The fastest skier wins the event.
- slalom, giant slalom, super giant slalom (Super G), in which skiers race down a course about .6 miles (1 kilometer) long, carving smooth, tight turns to zigzag around flags called gates set in the snow. Skiers must pass through all the gates trying not to knock them down. The fastest skier wins the event.
- alpine combined is an event in which skiers must complete two slalom races and a downhill race.

Slalom racers wear ski suits with some padding to protect them against hitting the gates.

Nordic skiing

Nordic events include cross-country skiing and ski jumping. In cross-country skiing events, competitors race across fields and through forests, over distances ranging from 3 to 31 miles (5 to 50 kilometers). The skiers take long steps as they slide across the snow on skis that are longer, thinner and lighter than those worn by alpine skiers. The boots are attached to the skis only at the toe to enable the skier to take long strides and glide across the snow.

In ski-jumping competitions, a skier speeds down a snow-covered ramp called the inrun, and jumps up and over a steep hill to become airborne.

Freestyle skiing

Freestyle skiing became an Olympic event in 1992. The two freestyle events are:

- moguls, in which competitors ski straight down the bumpy fall line, performing jumps and turns as often as possible. Judges award points for speed and for how well the skier jumps and turns.
- aerials, in which competitors take off from a ramp called the kicker, and perform twisting somersaults in midair.

ACTION FACT

Biathlon is a sport which combines cross-country skiing and rifle shooting. Competitors, carrying rifles, ski over a cross-country course, stopping at points along the way to shoot at targets.

Ski jumpers score points for the length of their jump.

Points are awarded for take-off, height, style and how well a somersault is performed in freestyle competition.

SKIING CHAMPIONS

Skiing is an ancient sport that has been developed over the years especially in those parts of the world where winters bring harsh, snowy conditions.

Champion male and female skiers of today have to be super fit and develop special skills for the various disciplines of skiing. Most of the top skiers come from countries in the west of Europe as well as the United States and Canada. World-standard competitions take place on most continents, and skiing is a major sport at the Winter Olympics.

↗ Renate Goetschl

- Born on June 8, 1975, Austria
- Began competitive skiing in 1981, at age 6
- Has competed in World Cup competitions since 1993

Career highlights

- Won five World Cup competitions in 1999
- Won six World Cup competitions in 2000
- Won three World Cup competitions in 2001
- Ranked second in the overall World Cup standings in 2001–2002
- Won a silver medal in Ladies' Combined and a bronze medal for the Ladies' Downhill competitions at Salt Lake City Winter Olympics in 2002
- Won four World Cup competitions in 2002

↗ Janica Kostelic

- Born May 1, 1982, Croatia
- First competed in the World Cup competition in 1998, finishing 12th
- Competed in her first Winter Olympics in 2002 and was named the outstanding female skier of the competition

Career highlights

- Won one World Cup competition in 1999
- Won two World Cup competitions in 2000
- Won nine World Cup competitions in 2001
- Won one World Cup competition in 2002
- Won a gold medal for Ladies' Combined, Giant Slalom and Ladies' Slalom, and a silver medal for Ladies' Super G competitions at the Salt Lake Winter Olympics in 2002

↗ Bart Bunting

- Born July 19, 1976, Australia
- Blind since birth
- Began competing in disabled skiing events in 1999
- Skis with the assistance of a guide, who skis 2 to 3 yards (2 to 3 meters) ahead, guiding him with a microphone in his helmet and a loudspeaker attached to the rear of his waist bag

Career highlights

- Won a gold medal in Men's Downhill and Men's Giant Slalom, fifth place in Men's Super G, and ninth place Men's Slalom at the World Championships in 2000
- Won a silver medal in Men's Super G and a bronze medal in Men's Downhill at the World Cup in 2001
- Won a gold medal in Men's Downhill and Men's Super G and a silver medal in Men's Giant Slalom at the Salt Lake City Paralympic Games in 2002

↗ Bode Miller

- Born October 12, 1977, United States
- Grew up in Franconia, New Hampshire, in a cabin without plumbing or heating
- Has reputation as skier who makes thrilling wins or who loses in spectacular crashes

Career highlights

- Won United States Giant Slalom Championship in 1998
- Won two World Cup events in 2001
- Won four World Cup victories, three in Slalom and one in the Giant Slalom, in the 2001–2002 World Cup season
- Won two silver medals in the Men's Giant Slalom and a silver medal in the Alpine Combined at the Salt Lake Winter Olympics in 2002

↗ Kjetil Andre Aamodt

- Born September 2, 1971, Norway
- Gained fame in 1990, when he won the Junior World Champion title in Downhill and Alpine Combined
- Has competed in four Winter Olympic Games

Career highlights

- Won a gold medal in Men's Super G and a bronze medal in Men's Giant Slalom competition at Albertville Winter Olympics in 1992
- Won a silver medal in Men's Giant Slalom and a bronze medal in Men's Super G competition at Lillehammer Winter Olympics in 1994
- Won one World Cup competition and reached the podium eight times in 1999
- Won three World Cup competitions in 2000 and two in 2002
- Ranked second in the overall World Cup standings in 2001–2002
- Won two gold medals at Salt Lake City Winter Olympics in 2002

1767–2000 THEN AND NOW

1767	1840	1904	1909	1922	1924	1936
Descriptions were written of professional skiing competitions in Norway.	Cross-country ski races were being held in Norway by military personnel.	The first ski book was written in English.	Kosciusko Alpine Club opened. It remains Australia's oldest, continuously operating ski club.	The first modern slalom race, the Alpine Ski Challenge Cup, was held at Mürren, Switzerland.	The first Olympic Winter Games were held at Chamonix, France, with nordic ski events only.	The chair lift was invented and built by Jim Curran, an engineer with the Union Pacific Railroad at Sun Valley in the United States.

1909

1936

| **1949** | **1952** | **1959** | **1960** | **1983** | **1988** | **2000** |

The first commercially successful aluminium skis were made and sold in the United States.

The first artificial snow was made at a resort in New York.

The first plastic ski boots became available.

The first successful fiberglass skis were made and sold.

The Super G competition was added to World Cup events.

The Super G was added to Olympic competition.

New "breathable" fabrics used by **NASA**'s astronauts were used to make waterproof and windproof ski clothes, to keep skiers warm but not hot.

1983

RELATED ACTION SPORTS

Snowboarding

Snowboarding is gliding over the snow with the feet strapped to a board. There are three main styles of snowboarding:

- alpine racing or slalom, in which snowboarders race down a hill or mountain, zigzagging and changing direction quickly to pass in and out of posts called gates.
- freestyle, which includes the halfpipe. Freestyle is an acrobatic form of snowboarding.
- freeriding, in which snowboarders explore parts of the countryside away from ski resorts.

Ski boarding

Using short, lightweight skis about 3 feet (90 centimeters) long, ski boarders can move forward, backward and sideways. Like skateboarders, they jump and somersault in the halfpipe and grind and slide along rails. Ski-boarding events became part of the Winter X Games in 1998.

Snow mountain biking

Using mountain bikes fitted with metal-studded tyres, six riders race each other down a 300-meter icy track which features banked turns, called berms, and jumps. The Biker X competition event was first featured at the Australian Winter X Games in 1999.

Freestyle snowboarders perform tricks and jumps on flat ground or in a halfpipe cut into the snow.

Collisions and falls are common, so riders in Biker X events wear helmets and other protective gear.

GLOSSARY

carbon fiber a rigid but light substance used to make skis and ski poles

downhill the longest and fastest alpine-skiing event, comprised of one run, with the fastest time determining the winner

edges hard metal strips on either side of the skis

fall line the shortest and most direct line down a ski slope

freestyle skiing acrobatic skiing that includes moguls, jumps and aerial tricks, such as twists and somersaults

gates flags or plastic poles placed in the snow to mark the course for a slalom event

moguls also referred to as bumps, these are dome-shaped mounds skiers maneuver around or jump off of as they ski down a slope

NASA National Aeronautic and Space Administration in the United States

piste French word meaning "groomed ski runs at a resort"

polyethylene a type of plastic used on the base of skis

polyurethane a rigid, synthetic substance used to make ski boot shells

slalom an event in which competitors ski down a slope, in and out of "gates"

tail the rear end of a ski

tips the upward curve at the front end of the skis

wax a substance applied to the base of skis, used for increased control, speed and glide

INDEX

A
Aamodt, Kjetil Andre 27
aerials 5, 25
alpine skiing 5, 24
artificial snow 29
avalanches 13

B
biathlon 25
bindings 8
boots 9
Bunting, Bart 27

C
carving 21
chair lift 22, 23, 28
clothing 10–11
competitions 24–25
cross-country skiing 5, 25
Curran, Jim 28

F
falling 16
Fédération Internationale de Ski (FIS) 24
first-aid kit 13
fitness 13
free skiing 5
freestyle skiing 5, 25

G
Goetschl, Renate 26
Goldberger, Andreas 24

H
herringbone step 15
history 4, 28–29
hypothermia 11

K
Kostelic, Janica 26

M
maps 23
Miller, Bode 27
moguls 5, 25

N
nordic skiing 5, 25

O
Olympic skiing 24–25, 26, 27
Paralympic Games 27

R
resorts 22–23

S
safety 11, 12–13
safety signs 12
schussing 19
sideslipping 21
side-stepping 15
ski boarding 30
Ski Dome 23
skills and techniques 14–21
ski maintenance 7
ski poles 8
skis 6–7
slalom 5, 24, 29
snowboarding 30
snow mountain biking 30
snowplowing 18
sunscreen 11

T
T-Bar ski lift 23
traversing 20
turning 17, 21

W
walking on skis 14
warming up 13